Contemporary Hispanic Americans

NELY GALAN

BY
JANEL RODRIGUEZ

RSVP
RAINTREE
STECK-VAUGHN
P U B L I S H E R S
The Steck-Vaughn Company

Austin, Texas

Published by Raintree Steck-Vaughn, an imprint of Steck-Vaughn Company.
Produced by Mega-Books, Inc.
Design and Art Direction by Michaelis/Carpelis Design Associates.
Cover photo: Courtesy of BUZZ Magazine

Library of Congress Cataloging-in-Publication Data
Rodriguez, Janel.
  Nely Galan/by Janel Rodriguez.
    p.   cm. — (Contemporary Hispanic Americans)
  Includes bibliographical references (p. 47) and index.
    Summary: A biography of the young Cuban-American woman who rapidly moved from high school student to magazine editor to president of her own television production company.
  ISBN 0-8172-3991-X (Hardcover)
  ISBN 0-8172-6880-4 (Softcover)
  1. Galan, Nely 1963–   —Juvenile literature.
2. Television producers and directors—United States—Biography—Juvenile literature.
3. Hispanic American television producers and directors—Biography—Juvenile literature.
[1. Galan, Nely, 1963—.   2. Television producers and directors.
3. Cuban Americans—Biography. 4. Women—Biography.]
I. Title.   II. Series.
PN1998. 3. G33R64   1997
791.45'023'092—dc21   96-46944
[B]   CIP
                                                                AC

Printed and bound in the United States.

1 2 3 4 5 6 7 8 9 LB 00 99 98 97 96

Photo credits: Courtesy of Nely Galan: pp. 4, 7, 8, 10, 13, 14, 17, 18, 21, 22, 24, 27, 29, 30, 33, 35, 38, 41, 44; ©1996 USA TODAY: p. 37; AP/Wide World Photos, Inc.: p. 42.

Contents

Chapter One

"HELLO. I'M NELY GALAN."

"Quiet on the set!"
"Cállate, por favor!"

It was 1994. In the lobby of a famous Hollywood restaurant, workers scrambled to get out of the way of the television camera. A petite woman in a designer suit joked with the cameraman while adjusting her skirt. Her name was Nely Galan. The director of "The Gossip Show" gave the word. "Action!" The camera zoomed in on Nely, getting a close-up of her pretty, smiling face.

"Hello," she said. "I'm Nely Galan."

At first glance Nely might look like just another pretty face hosting a television show. But she wasn't then, and she isn't now. With her straight, thick hair

Nely Galan, one of the most powerful executives in the field of broadcasting, is dedicated to bringing Latino cultures into the mainstream of American media.

and her bright, brown eyes, Nely's image has smiled out at millions of TV viewers all over the country for years.

Nely's career started early. She was the host of a television news program for teenagers when she was only 18 years old. Later Nely hosted her own talk show, called "Bravo." She worked for the cable network E! on its program, "The Gossip Show." Nely has also hosted, cohosted, or guest-hosted dozens of other shows. Time and again her friendly face has greeted viewers with the words, "Hello. I'm Nely Galan."

But who is Nely Galan? She is more than just a talking head in front of a camera. In fact Nely is most famous for her work as a businesswoman behind the scenes of **broadcasting**. *Entertainment Weekly* magazine wrote that Nely is "one of the most powerful young executives in Hollywood, California." Nely is also sometimes called "the Cuban Missile." It is a nickname that came about because of her focus and determination to be successful.

Nely is exactly that—a success story. At present Nely is a busy Hollywood **producer**. She heads her own production company called gaLAn entertainment, which is named after her. A producer's job is sort of like being a chef. Chefs use lots of ingredients to create a meal. A producer brings together many talented people, such as writers, directors, actors, and camera operators, to create a movie or television show.

Being a producer means having a lot of responsibility. In that way Nely is like every other

Nely (center), with the staff of her production company, gaLAn entertainment, works to see that Latinos are represented fairly in all media, from TV and film to books and music.

producer. But in some ways, Nely stands apart from other producers. She is special because she is three things most producers are not: she is young, she is a woman, and she is Latina. (Latina means a woman who has a Spanish-speaking cultural background, while a man of Spanish or South American heritage is called Latino. A group of these men and women together are called Latinos.)

"I love being Latina," Nely has said. "It is my greatest asset and the key to my career." To Nely her heritage is her best feature. Nely's goal from an early age was to work in the entertainment industry, but she didn't always know where she would fit in. It was only when Nely tapped into her culture that she discovered her place in the entertainment business.

One day while watching TV, Nely realized something very important. It occurred to her that there were Spanish-language programs on Spanish channels for Latinos. However, there weren't any programs about Latinos on English-language channels. There weren't any shows for Latinos who, like Nely, had been raised in the United States and could speak English. It was as though Latinos didn't exist in the world of television.

This realization was like a wake-up call for Nely. At that moment she decided that she was going to develop television and video projects that were aimed

A good business sense combined with her creative flair has allowed Nely to go far in a short time and has earned her the nickname "the Cuban Missile."

toward Latino and Latino-American audiences. Nely didn't want to take what was already on Spanish TV and just translate it into English. She wanted to create something different. She wanted to develop shows that could ". . .reach my mother in Spanish and me in English."

Nely's instincts about what was missing from television made her a pioneer of sorts. She became a new face on a frontier of television that had yet to be explored. Also like a pioneer, Nely had the strength and courage to meet head-on the challenges that would come her way.

When other people found out about Nely's television and video projects, she was suddenly in demand. It turned out that other people were thinking the same way as Nely, only they didn't know where to start. Nely had the skills, background, talent, and vision to make it all work, and as a result, gaLAn entertainment was born.

As the president of her own company, Nely has a very active workday. During the day she rushes from one end of Los Angeles, California to another, in a hurry to get from meeting to meeting. The rest of the time she can be found in her office, talking on the phone. Even so there is always a very long list of phone messages from people trying to contact her. As a rule Nely always calls people back. After all, she can still remember how she felt when people in Hollywood didn't return her calls.

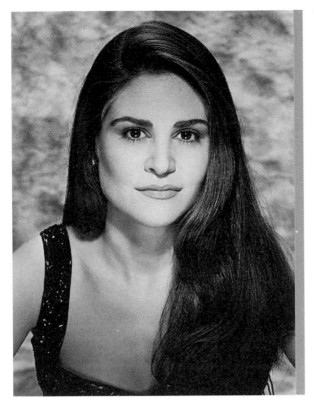

Whether she is hosting her own talk show or handling the details of producing a film project, Nely feels comfortable on both sides of the camera.

In the evening, when other people are heading home, Nely is still working. By then she is usually reading TV or movie scripts written from a Latino point of view. Nely is an energetic businesswoman who works hard because she wants everything to be just right.

There have been times in Nely's life, however, when things did not go "just right." Nely has had difficulty with her parents, has had to cancel shows, and has had a failed marriage. Yet somehow Nely made it through her problems. How did she do it? How did she become so strong? Nely can trace the source of her strength back to a time when she was 15 years old and attending an all-girls school. Up until that point, she had been a good student who always did her homework and never got in trouble. Nely even goes so far as to describe her past self as "wimpy." Suddenly the quiet girl found herself being unjustly accused of something she didn't do. "I became," Nely says, "a different person after that."

"BEING A WIMP DOESN'T PAY OFF."

When Nely was just a girl, she was nothing like the confident, take-charge kind of person she would later grow up to be. The story of Nely's change from a shy girl to a powerful businesswoman begins in the country of Cuba.

Cuba is a tropical island located in the Caribbean Sea between North and South America, just 90 miles from Key West, Florida. Cuba is a country of banana trees, cool breezes, and many beaches. Nely was born in Santa Clara, Cuba, on September 28, 1963. She was her parents' first child. Because of this her parents wanted to name her something special, so they combined their own first names, Arsenio and Nelida, and made up a new name: "Arnely." Unfortunately, their daughter didn't care for the name. "I hated it," Nely says. So she uses "Nely," a shortened version of the name.

As a toddler Nely was warmed by the love of her

Nely and her mother, Nelida, photographed in Cuba, where Nely was born. Nely's full name is Arnely Alvarez.

parents and the comfortable temperatures of the Cuban climate. However, there was another kind of climate on the island—one of political unrest. The island has been ruled by a dictator named Fidel Castro since 1959. Whatever he orders has to be followed, without question. Citizens of Cuba do not have the right to free speech like citizens of the United States. This means that a Cuban cannot speak out against the government, even if something seems unfair or wrong. To disagree or protest against Castro can mean prison, or even death.

Arsenio Alvarez decided that, even though Cuba was his homeland, it was no longer a safe place to raise his family. His wife, Nelida, needed some convincing, however. She was a rural schoolteacher and didn't want to leave without having someone to teach her students. Mrs. Alvarez also pointed out that Nely was just a baby and was too young to leave the country. By the time Mrs. Alvarez had made arrangements for her class, she was pregnant again, and Nely was two years old. In 1965, just two days after Nely's brother, Arsenio Alvarez, Jr., was born, the Alvarez family escaped to Spain. With the help of a program run by a Presbyterian church in the United

Arsenio and Nelida Galan, with their children Arsenio, Jr. and Nely, just after they moved to the United States.

States, Nely's family moved from Spain to the United States eight months later.

The Alvarez family settled in Teaneck, New Jersey. The street they lived on was quiet and lined with trees, but Nely and her family could not help feeling strange and lost. They were the only Latino family in the whole neighborhood. Most other people who had escaped from Cuba had settled in the state of Florida. Since Florida was so close to Cuba, Cubans could make it there by boat. Some Cubans even risked their lives by making the trip to freedom on rafts! As a result there were a lot of Spanish-speaking Cubans in Miami, but not in Teaneck, New Jersey.

Nely's parents could not speak English. They had a difficult time adjusting to their new land. Luckily Nely was young, and as the years passed she learned to master her second language with the help of television. Watching TV made it easier for Nely to pick up the language and customs of her new country. She soon had favorite programs like "The Brady Bunch" and "The Partridge Family." Nely's mother preferred to watch "Maria Teresa," which was a soap opera on a Spanish channel. Nely sometimes liked to make up a world of her own and imagine a place where the Bradys could live with Maria Teresa. She didn't know it then, but she was already beginning to think like a producer.

Meanwhile Nely's parents worked hard. Nely's mother could no longer be a teacher, because she only spoke Spanish. Mrs. Alvarez became a homemaker and a seamstress. As a seamstress she made money by sewing clothes for people in the neighborhood. Nely's father worked as a salesman for a food company that specialized in producing Spanish foods like rice, beans, and spices.

Nely was educated at Holy Angels Academy. The all-girls Catholic school was located in Demarest, New Jersey, not too far from Nely's home. Nely was an obedient student who always did her work on time. Her favorite subject was English. She always did well in English and enjoyed writing very much. When Nely was 15 years old, her English teacher asked the class to make up a short story for a creative writing assignment. After some thought, Nely had an idea. She wrote a story about a wealthy woman who dies. Instead of leaving her riches to her relatives to inherit, the woman leaves behind only a letter. The letter, her family discovers, is the woman's explanation of what she thinks life is all about. Nely handed in her finished story to the teacher with pride.

Nely was even prouder when her teacher returned the story. The teacher had given her the highest grade in the class! Nely couldn't believe it when the teacher chose to read her story out loud to the whole class. That week was one of the most thrilling in Nely's life.

But the next week, the very same teacher who had praised Nely's story changed her mind. The teacher decided that Nely had not actually written the story.

Nely was 15 and a high school sophomore when this picture was taken at a semiformal dance.

She felt that Nely was too young to have made it up on her own. She said that Nely must have copied the story from someone else.

Nely was devastated. The teacher had accused her of **plagiarism**. That meant the teacher thought Nely had written down, word for word, what another person had already had published. Plagiarism is stealing someone else's work.

Nely defended herself. Her parents stood by her. After a lot of discussion, Nely got an A on her paper. But she still wasn't satisfied. Nely wrote an essay called "Why You Should Never Send Your Kids to an All-Girls Catholic School" and sent it to *Seventeen* magazine. Although the magazine didn't publish her article, Nely was offered something even better. *Seventeen* asked her if she would like to be a guest editor.

Magazine editors oversee which articles are chosen for each month's issue. They decide which features to keep, which to postpone, and which not to use at all. Being a guest editor means being a substitute for the actual editor. It is an important position. For a short time, Nely was to take an editor's place at the magazine and help put out an issue for an upcoming month. It was a wonderful opportunity and "the best thing that ever happened to me," said Nely. Suddenly Nely was a new person, confident and strong.

Her own mother was shocked by the change. It was as if she no longer knew her own daughter. She began calling Nely "E.T." after the famous alien in the

Nely overcame a bad situation in school that landed her a job at *Seventeen* magazine. This was a turning point in her life that gave her the confidence to succeed.

movie of the same name, because "I figured she must be from outer space." Mrs. Alvarez also said that suddenly Nely "wasn't afraid of anything anymore."

Nely explains that she had "seen the light," and finally realized that "being a wimp doesn't pay off." She decided to take control of her life. She accepted a job at *Seventeen*. She also took on more classes in school, allowing her to graduate early. *Seventeen* was so pleased with her work that they decided to give her a permanent job. Nely quickly went from a high school graduate to a working woman who hired models for fashion shoots and wrote magazine articles. Nely was quite young. She celebrated her 16th birthday while working at *Seventeen*. A year later the Elite modeling agency hired Nely. There Nely helped models who pose for fashion magazines get work.

Meanwhile Nely's parents were confused by all that was happening. Their daughter was going places fast—too fast, in their opinion. When the Elite modeling agency wanted to send Nely to work at a fashion show in Paris, France, Nely's parents forbade her to go. Nely had to make a difficult decision. The "old" Nely would have done what her parents wished. But the "new" Nely saw that going to Europe was a great opportunity. So she decided to go to Paris.

Three

THE NEW NELY

Nely's parents "had a fit," as Nely explains. They thought that Nely should be working on her college degree or getting married. But Nely wanted to pursue her independence and freedom. She says she realized that she had "a destiny." She wanted to find out where it would lead her. There was no stopping her now.

Nely made sure that she kept in contact with her parents while she was in Paris. When she told them that she was staying in the home of a nice family, her parents calmed down a bit.

Nely's work for *Seventeen* led her to another job. A producer for PBS (the Public Broadcasting System) read some of Nely's articles. One of them really grabbed the producer's attention. The article was titled "Who Says Christie Brinkley Is Beautiful?" It was an intelligent article that questioned why blond hair, blue eyes, and other such features (like those of fashion model Christie Brinkley) were considered

By the time Nely was 17, she had gone to Paris to cover a fashion show for the Elite modeling agency.

beautiful in the American culture. Nely didn't think it was fair that people from Latin, Asian, or African backgrounds were judged by such standards. In the article she pointed out that there were many different kinds of physical beauty.

The producer decided to film a **documentary** on the same subject. A documentary is different from a regular movie. Movies usually tell a made-up story. Documentaries inform their viewers. They can be films about nature, or about important events, or just about real people in real-life situations. People in documentaries are usually not actors. They speak in their own words, not from memorized lines of a script. They also move naturally, wherever and whenever they wish, since their actions are not ordered by a director. Photographs and news clips, very short bits of film, are often used in documentaries as well. The producer who contacted Nely wanted this documentary to be a pilot—that is, the first episode of a film series for teens. The producer paid Nely $100 for the use of her article and invited Nely to join her in Texas.

Nely became the on-air reporter for the series, which was called "Checking It Out." Nely had never worked in front of a camera before, and moving to Texas was a big step. Not to mention that she was only 18 years old. Nely made the move, however. She realized that if there was one thing she had learned from sending in that first article to *Seventeen*

Nely Galan, pictured here with her fellow cast members, was the on-air reporter for the series "Checking It Out," a documentary news magazine aimed specifically at teens.

magazine, it was that sometimes "you have to take risks." Nely is glad she decided to take that risk, because it provided her with a solid foundation in the television business.

While in Texas Nely met many people in the film business. One of them was a Mexican-American documentary filmmaker, named Hector Galan. He was "a great guy," says Nely. "What I liked about him was that he was really good at what he did."

Hector was much older than Nely and was self-assured and talented. Nely admired him and hoped to be as good in her career as he was in his. After three months, the two were married. Nely Alvarez was now Nely Galan. At the time Nely thought she was doing the right thing. She knew that her parents wanted her to marry, and Hector seemed to be the right man. Unfortunately the marriage ended after only four years.

"I was too young," Nely says, looking back on those days. She had moved too fast when she still had a lot of growing up to do.

While Nely and Hector were still married, Nely got a call from television personality Geraldo Rivera. Nely had done some work for Mr. Rivera in the past, and he remembered how good she was. Mr. Rivera was working on a documentary in Boston, Massachusetts, and needed a producer for it. He asked Nely to send in a sample videotape of her work so that she could be considered for the job. However, Geraldo told Nely,

WHAT'S WRONG WITH THIS PICTURE?

Nely felt like she was in the middle of nowhere, with no future. However, at the age of 22, she was the youngest television station manager in the country. In spite of how Nely felt at the time, she was actually doing quite well. Soon Nely's enthusiasm for her new job began to grow, little by little. As she watched shows her station was putting on the air, Nely had what she called, "a religious experience."

"Something is wrong with this picture," Nely thought to herself, and she couldn't rest until she put her finger on it. Then one day she realized what was wrong. Many of the programs had nothing to do with Latinos who were brought up in the United States as children. The shows were really developed for her mother's generation.

People Nely's age and younger seemed to be "like a lost generation," Nely has said. The shows weren't

Nely's goal was to develop shows for her generation of Hispanics brought up in the United States. She wanted to produce English shows that all Latinos would watch.

even produced in the United States. They were filmed in places like Central and South America. Spanish TV producers were not the only ones forgetting a large part of their audience. There were hardly any Latino people on regular American programs. "We're not on American TV. We're not on Spanish TV. Nobody sees us anywhere," said Nely. "When I'm my mother's age," she realized, "I won't be watching Spanish TV but Hispanic TV that's in English." Now all she had to do was figure out what she was going to do with her new ideas.

The first thing Nely decided was that if she was going to have any influence on television, she had to really know what she was doing. She threw herself into her job and worked hard at running WNJU-TV. To her surprise she enjoyed herself immensely. She had discovered what she was going to do with her life.

Work actually became fun. She learned a lot and made friends. She was also surrounded by many Latino cultures, which she found she loved. "Each Latin nation has its own set of rules, its own culture," Nely noticed. But she also knew that all those different cultures had many things in common. After all, the rest of the United States, which was made up of non-Latino people from all over the world, could watch the same television shows and relate to them. Nely was determined to create programs that all Latinos— as well as everyone else in the United States—would relate to, together.

It was a very exciting, hope-filled time in her life. After three great years, the station was sold, and Nely was very sad. The time spent at the station had been some of the best moments of her life. Now that the station was sold, however, Nely could put her ideas to the test. It was time for her to create a new kind of television program for a new kind of audience.

In 1988 Nely had a big break. She was asked to host and produce her own talk show. It was called "Bravo." The show was a half-hour long and was filmed at the WCAU-TV studios in Philadelphia, Pennsylvania. What was special about the program was that it was filmed in both English and Spanish. For Hispanic TV to be truly for Hispanic Americans, Nely thought, it would have to be available in both languages. "Just English or just Spanish is for the birds," she decided. For her vision of what television should be, Nely knew that both audiences needed to be reached at the same time.

The two versions of Nely's show were sold to stations all over the country, and both of them aired. The show did very well, reaching over half of all Hispanic households in the United States. What was even more surprising was that it reached over 32 percent of total households in the country. This meant that non-Latinos were watching. Not only that, but the English version of Nely's show was watched more than the Spanish version. The very audience that Nely wanted to reach was responding.

What made it all the better was that "Bravo"

"Bravo," Nely's show that was filmed in Spanish and English, was the first of its kind to focus on a young Latino audience. Here she interviews the designer Isabel Toledo.

focused on the achievements of Latinos. Nely interviewed many of the leaders, actors, musicians, and influential people of the Latino community. Different programs found Nely sitting opposite such stars as Edward James Olmos, Gloria Estefan, and Jimmy Smits. As Nely interviewed these and other famous people, she started to become famous herself.

At the age of 26, Nely was already changing the face of television. Magazine and newspaper reporters

Jimmy Smits and Jenifer Lopez with Nely (left) at the Bravo Awards, for which she was the executive producer.

were interested in what she had to say. It was strange for Nely, who made a living through interviewing others, to suddenly become the person others wanted to interview. Nely was becoming a star in her own right. In fact, after a while, the format of the show was changed to highlight its host more. The name of the talk show was even changed to "Nely"—the same way other talk shows like "Oprah" and "Donahue" were named after their star hosts.

Even though she was successful, Nely wasn't truly happy. When Nely's show was canceled, she was actually a bit relieved. Her talk show experience had taught her something very important. "It was another turning point in my life," Nely says. Nely realized she wanted to be her own boss. She knew that in order to achieve her dream, she would have to run her own company. But there was a lot of work to do. Nely had already begun to make her mark. The next question was: What should be her next move?

Three major broadcast networks—ABC, CBS, and NBC—sought Nely's talent. She helped them all by either hosting, producing, or consulting, which means she gave advice and guidance. She also did work for cable channels. Concepción Lara, a friend of Nely's who worked at Home Box Office (HBO), got Nely a job working for the sports channel ESPN. Nely helped ESPN develop a Spanish sports channel. She knew that if she was going to make an impact on Latino television, she had to get involved in the way sports events and their players were covered.

ESPN was already broadcasting its English-only channel in Spanish-speaking countries when Nely was called in to help. ESPN producers wanted to create a sports channel in Spanish to reach a wider audience. Nely says, "American sports make no sense to Latin Americans." When football games were shown on the channel, a **voice-over** had to explain the rules of the game. An unexpected hit with the Latin American audience was hockey. The only problem with showing the games on the new channel was figuring out a Spanish word for "puck." There is no translation for the disklike object that players try to hit or slide into opposing teams' nets. After many long meetings and discussions, it was eventually decided to continue using the word "puck."

While doing all of these things, sometimes Nely would get frustrated. When would her dream come true? She was making progress, she knew, but things did not always move fast enough for Nely. When she was tired, she sometimes discussed her problem with her friend Concepción Lara, who had helped her get the job with ESPN. Like Nely, Concepción was born in a Spanish-speaking country (Mexico) and had moved to the United States (California) with her family as a child. Both she and Nely were in the television business, and both of them were women. They had a lot in common. It was no wonder they were friends. The two women agreed that it would only be a matter

Nely Galan and her close friend Concepción Lara, an executive at HBO who changed the way American channels were broadcast in Spanish-speaking countries.

of time before Latinos would get their chance to make it on American television. Nely didn't know how soon that chance would come.

HBO, the company Concepción worked for, wanted Nely's help. They wanted to create a new show about growing up Latino in the United States. The company needed a producer of Latino background and with experience in the television business to make it work. Nely's name came up as the perfect choice. Her past work for HBO had made a great impression. Nely was glad. Now she hoped a job with the cable network would be her chance to make her ideas a reality. All she needed to do was to convince HBO.

"YOU CAN'T GIVE UP."

HBO wanted to create a situation comedy (or sitcom) about the Latino-American experience. Nely was asked to create a half-hour show. Nely decided to write about what had happened to her when she was accused of plagiarism in high school. It made an interesting story, and it felt good to get that terrible incident out of her system.

HBO liked the script very much. After a few negotiations with Nely, the production company Tropix was created in 1992. Now the Latino division of HBO had a name. As cofounder of the company, Nely could work with HBO to put Latino faces on cable television. Nely felt that many of the Latino youth of America were damaged by not being able to identify with the people they saw on television. They had "no role models . . .and that reflects badly on their self-esteem," she once said. Nely was determined to repair that damage.

Nely produced a series of comedy specials that ran for four weeks on HBO. It was called "Loco Slam." The series showcased Latino and Latino-American comics and humor. The host of the show was a comedian named Carlos Mencia. Another famous Hispanic comedian, Paul Rodriguez, also helped produce the show with Nely. "Loco Slam" did well in the ratings, and Nely was on her way to becoming a successful television producer.

While at HBO Nely and close friend Paul Rodriguez produced a comedy series called "Loco Slam," which featured Latino comedians.

She began to oversee many different projects, including a three-hour special about the Latino family experience. What made the project interesting was that each hour was dedicated to a different Latino culture: the Puerto Rican experience in America, the Cuban experience in America, and the Mexican experience in America. Nely made sure that Puerto Rican, Cuban, and Mexican writers were chosen to work on the show. She wanted the program to be as true to real life as possible.

Nely also worked with Concepción Lara on creating the graphics for the Fox Latin American Channel. The graphics are the pictures, symbols, and logo (usually the name of a company) that flash across the screen and inform the viewer which station they are watching. Nely did some research before coming up with ideas. She discovered a survey that had asked Latinos what they valued most in life. In order of importance, the first three choices were as follows: love, family, and career. With love being the most important, Nely knew the channel would have to look beautiful, sensual, and richly colored. She approached the award-winning graphics agency of Pittard Sullivan Fitzgerald. Using "hot" colors, like those seen in a desert sunrise, they came up with designs of scarlet roses, glittery veils, and banners that billowed in the wind. Their logo for Fox resembled an ancient South American pyramid.

The design was used in the video spots for station

Nely feels that the look of each show—eye-catching graphics and bold, "hot" colors—is an important factor in attracting viewers of all ages.

identification. This was done by showing a quick clip of the beautiful graphics and logo during commercial breaks. They looked fantastic, and the audience responded well to them. So did the Broadcast Designers Association, which awarded its 1994 Gold Award to the video spots, voting them the best out of over 40 other entries from around the world.

Finally Nely was getting the recognition that all her years of hard work had called for. Early on Nely

When Nely hosted the "Gossip Show," she included news about well-known Latino stars, such as Rosie Perez.

had known that "you have to have patience. You can't give up." She was glad that she had kept focused on her goal. That's what had made it a reality. Nely also realized that she could not just sit back and admire what she had done. She had to keep working.

In 1993 the E! Entertainment Network needed a host for "The Gossip Show" at the last minute. Someone had to take the place of Joan Rivers. Nely, who was young, pretty, and had experience in front of a camera, was offered the job. "No," a busy Nely answered at first. That is, until she saw another opportunity. She decided to take the job, but only if the cable channel would develop a Spanish version of the show as well. Nely knew that Latinos would be interested in Hollywood gossip. After all, American movies always did well in Latin America. Nely made sure, however, that the latest news on Latino movie and TV stars were also included. Sure enough the Spanish version of the show later on proved to be just as popular as the original English one.

Some people said that Nely was spreading herself too thin. They thought that she was involved in too many projects at the same time. Nely disagreed. "It's good that I do too many things," she said. "It's what saves me." Nely felt secure knowing how to do so many jobs. That way she would never be out of work in a business she loved so much. Her work had become her life.

Although she was busy and successful, Nely still wasn't satisfied. She had to decide what her next step would be. She wanted to continue working in television, but she didn't want to be limited to only television. She realized Latinos needed support in other areas as well. They weren't just missing from American television. Latinos were missing from books, music, and the movies, too. Nely wanted to produce them all. The people at Fox Television were thinking the same way. They noticed Nely's dedication to her cause and to her culture. In the fall of 1994, Nely made a deal with Fox. News of the deal quickly hit the Hollywood papers.

gaLAn
ENTERTAINMENT

"**G**ALAN INKS PACT WITH FOX TV" read the headline of the article in *Daily Variety*. "FOX GOING AFTER LATINO AUDIENCE" was the title of the article in *Electronic Media* magazine. The *Hollywood Reporter* read, "FOX, GALAN PACT FOR HISPANIC TV." The deal was also reported in the *Los Angeles Times* and in the *Wall Street Journal*. David Evans, the president of Fox Television, happily announced the deal saying, "Nely's reputation as a producer and TV executive is unmatched."

Nely was finally where she wanted to be. She had made it. She was now in a position to produce both English and Spanish television for audiences in the United States and Latino countries. She could also produce movies, music, and more in English and Spanish. She was president of a company that was even named after her: gaLAn entertainment. The "L" and the "A" in her name are capitalized to highlight the

Nely (left), with Fox owner, Rupert Murdoch, and Concepción Lara during the launch of the new Fox network for Latin America.

fact that the company is based in Los Angeles, California.

Today Nely is working on that goal as well as all her other production responsibilities. She has already produced a novella called "Empire." (A novella is a Spanish-style soap opera.) But "Empire" is in English. It's the first of its kind ever to be made for television and will soon be seen on TV.

Nely has involved gaLAn entertainment in many projects. The company plans to make a film about the life of Hall-of-Fame baseball player Roberto

Clemente. The Puerto Rican baseball star died in a plane crash while on his way to help save Nicaraguans who had been in an earthquake.

Nely also continues to help launch new channels into Latin America, such as Fox Kids and Fox Sports. Nely plans to write a self-help book for Latina women and is working on a deal with a major

Dedicated to bringing awareness of Latino heroes from all fields to the public eye, Nely is planning a film about baseball Hall-of-Famer Roberto Clemente.

publishing house to produce books with Latino themes by Latino writers.

Nely explains what she's doing: "The aim of gaLAn entertainment is to become a cultural bridge between the United States and Latin America. Not only will we tailor and produce quality programming for the Latin American market, we will also take genres (or styles) that are staples of Latin American television and adapt them for the American mainstream. This is a totally new and exciting concept for American television."

Aside from her work as a producer, Nely expresses herself in other creative ways. She wrote a play called *Mi Dulce Tormento*. It is the story of a mother and a daughter who have a communication problem. Then the daughter travels back in time to the year 1950. There she meets her mother who is the same age she is. The daughter realizes that she and her mother are a lot alike. This realization makes her fear that she's going to be just like her mother when she grows older. The play was performed on stage in Los Angeles by the Bilingual Foundation for the Arts.

Nely is also a member of The National Board of the Smithsonian Institution. Just in her early 30s, she is more than 20 years younger than anyone else on the board. Nely wants to make sure that Latino cultures are represented fairly. Being on the board is another great way for Nely to achieve her goal of mainstreaming Hispanic cultures in the United States.

Nely received the National Hispanic Leadership Fellowship from Harvard University. Here she meets another role model, First Lady Hillary Rodham Clinton.

In other words she wants the average American to have an acceptance and understanding of what the Latino experience is all about. "There aren't a lot of people who have the unique experience of understanding two different worlds," Nely once said.

Nely was recently chosen to receive the National Hispanic Leadership Fellowship by Harvard University's John F. Kennedy School of Government. She is the only person on the list whose work is neither in government nor education. But by reaching out to Latinos of different countries and backgrounds,

Nely's work has always been educational.

Nely is now the executive producer of the Bravo Awards, which first aired on television in December of 1995. Nely plans to continue producing the show once a year. It is very special to her because it is a show that honors the achievements of Latinos in the entertainment business.

With all that Nely does at once, it is easy to see that she enjoys hard work. But she is not all work and no play. Nely admits she also enjoys fashion. "When you're Latina, you're always into clothes. You're raised to care about clothes and how you look. It's your culture," she says. "With the work I do, it's very important that I make a statement. You want your clothes to say something about how you think, how you run your business, who you are."

For all her accomplishments, Nely is not always seen as a success in her family circle because "I'm not married, and I don't have a child." She understands that Latinas are usually expected to be married and mothers by the age of 30. Not so for American women. Sometimes the two cultures of Nely's world clash. For the most part, Nely doesn't let that bother her. She says, "I am very secure about who I am and what I know. Ultimately I've done the work, and I have the skills." In the end Nely knows, "My work will speak for itself."

1963   Born Arnely Alvarez in Santa Clara, Cuba, on
        September 28.

1965   Nely's family escapes to Spain from Cuba.

1966   The Alvarez family settles in Teaneck, New Jersey.

1979   Nely is wrongly accused of plagiarism while a student
        in high school. *Seventeen* magazine asks Nely to be a
        guest editor when she is only 15 years old.

1981   Eighteen-year-old Nely moves to Texas and hosts
        her first television program, called "Checking It Out,"
        for PBS. Marries Hector Galan.

1985   At 22, Nely divorces Hector and becomes the
        youngest television station manager in the United
        States for WNJU-TV, in Linden, New Jersey.

1988   Hosts "Bravo," her own successful talk show. Later
        the name of the show is changed to "Nely."

1992   Works for HBO and helps to create a new production
        company called Tropix.

1994   In a deal with Fox, becomes head of gaLAn
        entertainment, a production company that promises
        modern entertainment for Latino audiences.

Glossary

broadcasting   The business of transmitting radio or television shows through airwaves and into the homes of listeners and viewers.

documentary   A film or television program that presents and discusses real news events, ideas, or a person's life.

plagiarism   Copying or taking another person's ideas or writings and presenting them as one's own.

producer   A person who makes a movie or show ready for release or performance by bringing together money, people, and ideas.

voice-over   The voice of an unseen person who announces or narrates a film or television program.

Bibliography

Marich, Robert. *The Hollywood Reporter*. September 27, 1994.

Paxman, Andrew. *Daily Variety*. September 27, 1994.

Rodriguez, Janel. Personal interview with Nely Galan. April 1996.

Walley, Wayne. *Electronic Media*. October 3, 1994.

Index